SHARD IN THE HEART

Survival Poetry

By

Ellen Clarke

ISBN: 978-1-956603-01-9

"I know what it's like: that ever-present hole of bitter darkness, gnawing at your heart. That ache of wanting to reach out for someone to hold, knowing they're gone forever, and then...and then… when I walked in here and saw all of you,

I wanted to leap for joy, to cry, to hug you all, and to never let you leave my sight again. The pain that has been in my heart since I lost every single one of you has been nearly unbearable but bear it I did. And I will continue to do so.

You're right, Kristen, I'm not the Maddy you knew. Just like you're not the sister I knew and loved, the sister who saved my life when she forced me to make a promise over a borrowed jacket."

(Battalion-13)

Shard in the Heart

Dedication

Sarah Elliot, my AP English teacher helped me stage a revolution on the last day of high school. The head teacher decided that my poem, which contained the word "bitch" was inappropriate and made her rip that page out of the literary magazine. I hadn't realized my poem would be published because I had submitted it anonymously, but Sarah knew and showed me the pile of freshly torn pages. The poem I wrote was only a small section on the page; half of a classmate's story was completed on the other side. I couldn't let my vulgar poem, inspired by my alcoholic mother, be the reason that other works wouldn't be enjoyed- or even finished. I grabbed the pile, headed to the busses, and passed out the pages, letting everyone know that student's work was being censored. This compilation contains poetry written in the blank book that Sarah gifted me before graduation over 20 years ago when I made her a promise to never stop writing. Simple acts of inspiration are life changing. Thank you for giving me a platform to spew forth my protests. I refuse to give up. I refuse to surrender. I refuse to stop writing.

.

Table of Contents

Introduction

We are born into this world without understanding that the circumstances around us will inevitably cause heartache. Heartache forms a dark shard that grows until we either die of a broken heart or seek help. I wrote until I gained freedom from that shard in my heart.

"Shard in My Heart" is born of the idea that multiple versions of oneself exist. Every time you make a decision, another version of you makes the opposite choice. There are versions of us that have lost their lives to suicide.

When suicide occurs, there's so much pain that the soul shatters and splits into shards. These painful shards are embedded into the living versions of the soul. Those of us who exist must bear the pain and carry on even though we do not understand why our heart aches.

The poems in this compilation were born of a need to spill my frustration onto pages and away from my heart. My greatest hope is that by sharing my words, you can relate to my stories and find a way out of the darkness, a way to pull the shard out of your heart. Open your heart, pour out the words and experience life.

Alcoholics

"I don't want to be the filler if the void is solely yours
I don't want to be your glass of single malt whiskey
Hidden in the bottom drawer
I don't want to be a bandage if the wound is not mine
Lend me some fresh air"

(Morrisette)

Shard in the Heart

I Dream to Escape

I dream.

I dream to escape the pressures of life.

I dream of gorgeous guys on a movie screen.

I dream of hot air balloons: red, white, and green.

I dream to forget strife.

To escape where I don't want to be.

I came home and slept because I am sad.

I get home and lay down; the bitch is mad.

Oh shame, shame, I didn't clean my room.

You ask me, "What problems do teenage girls have except teenage boys?"

I say who doesn't have problems when all parents are assholes and bitches.

I dream.

I dream to escape the pressures of life.

I dream of gorgeous guys on a movie screen.

I dream of hot air balloons: red, white, and green.

I dream to forget strife.

To escape where I don't want to be.

Shard in the Heart

So, I finally get to dream and what do I hear?

Another bitch at the door spoiling another dream.

I need to escape.

I run so far.

But it is only in my dream that I achieved my escape.

I dream.

I dream to escape the pressures of life.

I dream of gorgeous guys on a movie screen.

I dream of hot air balloons: red, white, and green.

I dream to forget strife.

To escape where I don't want to be.

"Clean your room slut."

"Clean your room bitch."

"Clean your room lazy."

"Clean your room witch."

I dream.

I dream to escape the pressures of life.

I dream of gorgeous guys on a movie screen.

I dream of hot air balloons: red, white, and green.

Shard in the Heart

I dream to forget strife.

To escape where I don't want to be.

So, I do and then I dream.

I dream of purple mountains where justice is prevailed.

I dream of Martin Luther King Jr. democracies.

I dream of a perfect world, the utopian society.

I dream of peace in all nations.

I dream . . . to escape.

Shard in the Heart

Will I?

If I should cage myself in

Like an animal,

Would I feel safe?

Or should I runaway,

To a freedom of poverty

Would I feel secure?

I only want to seek a refuge,

From an awful temper

Will I ever?

Shard in the Heart

When I Was Seven

When I was 7 my mom used to take us to the park.

When I was 7 my mom used to take my brother and I to the park to feed the ducks.

When I was 7 my mom used to take my brother and I to feed the ducks and we'd pick up fried chicken on the way.

When I was 7 my mom used to take my brother and I to feed the ducks and we'd pick up fried chicken on the way and mom would order a cup of ice.

When I was 7 my mom used to take my 3-year-old brother and I to feed the ducks and we'd pick up fried chicken on the way and mom would order a cup of ice and pour two beers into the cup.

When I was 7 my mom used to drive to the park drunk and drink on the way there. By the time we got home, we were out of chicken and beer.

Shard in the Heart

Dirty Laundry

Mother said you don't talk about your dirty laundry.

Later, I learned dirty laundry was my mom's brother molesting her.

Silence is deadly.

Shard in the Heart

Bullet in the Chamber

There's a bullet in the chamber and I can't sleep a wink,
Can't sleep a wink,
Can't sleep a wink.

There's a bullet in the chamber and it causes him to drink,
Causes him to drink,
Causes him to drink,

There's a bullet in the chamber and he doesn't love his wife,
Doesn't love his wife,
Doesn't love his wife,
Hasn't most his life.

There's a bullet in the chamber and she won't leave him either,
I'd rather fight than grieve her,
She does what she thinks is right.

There's a bullet in the chamber and he wants to see the light.

Shard in the Heart

Depression

"We'll carry on
And though you're broken and defeated
Your weary widow marches on"

(MCR)

Shard in the Heart

Chains

To the unholy demons watching over me,
Help me kill you so I may prosper.
Reign over the frustration that you give me,
Release these ropes tied around these wrists of mine.
Let me run unchained and unbound away from your
weights.
I love you,
So let me go.

Shard in the Heart

Deep

It's like falling
DEEP
Into a spell.

Pressure on my heart,
No one can escape.
Similar to dying,

Much worse than crying,
Depression is the worst.
We all wear black frowns.

Shard in the Heart

Sitting Alone

I'm sitting alone.
Tired of crying
Weary of being put aside.

Aye, your kisses are enthusiastic,
Hugs are so sincere,
Laughter so heartwarming-

But I'm here!
Sitting alone . . .
I need you!
I'm envious of her.
I feel rejected,
Weeping and sitting alone.

So long since our start,
I've sobbed excessively.
Why, why am I sitting alone?

Only togetherness
Will result in
Eternal happiness.

No weeping-
No sadness-
No sitting alone.

Now unite and
Be together forever
Forever is now.

Shard in the Heart

Comfort, Stability & Happiness

Why in a world so vast,
Is there no one to rely on?
I want stability, comfort & happiness.
When I find it, it's only temporary.

Have you ever had a fantasy,
Walk into your life,
Charm the pants off you,
And then walk out?

You always think that,
You've found the one,
The one that will cherish
You forever

You don't know what happened
You do, but you deny it
Faced with all the opportunities of the world,
You can't find them

This is what all of us search for
Only few are lucky enough to find it
Stability, comfort & happiness
Are the only true joys.

Shard in the Heart

Friendship

Lăotóng: (n.) lit. "old sames," a form of friendship between two 'heart sisters' – two women who are bound together in friendship tighter than Chinese foot bindings. Matched by astrological profiles, their pairing is like mandarin ducks is stronger than marriage.

(Various, Laotong)

Shard in the Heart

My Laotong

Were you the one disguised as soul sister?

Did you realize that your actions spoke louder than words?

We were not matched – not as we thought.

Too much yin in our friendship, not enough yang.

Our fireworks were not enough to keep us in deep heart love.

We never had a secret fan or even a book of shadows.

Our separations caused grief,

But this last time . . .

This last time . . .

I felt free.

Shard in the Heart

Slander

I ain't no Hollaback girl.

I wasn't happy to talk about you.

It's an intervention bitch.

Your husbands in a ditch.

I'll be a BLUR adapting,

Releasing hot hits.

You'll be the prude in blue,

With nothing left to do.

Don't hold back,

I'm doing just fine.

My dreams are coming true,

I don't need you.[i]

Shard in the Heart

Reaction to Rejection

One day she was my best friend,

The next, she was not.

I just arrived, after my date.

He said, "She does nay wanna speak to ya."

It was the worst rejection I have ever experienced.

Maybe he made her do it.

He never did like me.

He felt that our friendship ruined,

His and Hers,

Lost and gone forever.

I don't know what happened.

We were best friends.

We told each other everything.

She knew how I felt.

I knew how she felt.

Shard in the Heart

There was a psychic ability between us.

I could read hers and her mine.

As soon as the separation took place.

All was lost forever.

I'm not sad, just MT.[ii]

Frostburg Freaks

Harem
Witchcraft
Predatory

Manipulation
Deception
Games

Divide
Anger
Ruin

Breakup
Breakout
Alone

Shard in the Heart

Heartache

"You fit into me

like a hook into an eye

a fish hook

an open eye"

(Atwood)

Shard in the Heart

♪♪ Not So Good ♪♪

Seein' somethin' in a negative

Remindin' you of the good 'ol days

Wishin' you could be back there now

Chorus:

But you know . . .

It wouldn't be so good as you remember

Cos you forgot all the bad 'cept the weather

And you need the people you remember

And they're all gone on with their lives

Seein' somethin' on a yellowed page

Brings you back to the good 'ol days

Wanna go there now if I could

Chorus:

But you know . . .

It wouldn't be so good as you remember

Cos you forgot all the bad 'cept the weather

Shard in the Heart

And you need the people you remember

And they're all gone on with their lives

Cryin' now just remembering'

Need to go 'cos I can't see straight

Just hold on, I need a friend today

Chorus:

But you know . . .

It wouldn't be so good as you remember

Cos you forgot all the bad 'cept the weather

And you need the people you remember

And they're all gone on with their lives

If I could . . .

But you know . . .

It's not soooooo gooood.

The Offense

What will this world be …

When I drip blood from

Their necks,

When I throttle their throats.

When I smash their heads into the

Goddam window.

The Goddamned sidewalk.

I am so strong.

I can handle a fight.

Put your dukes up.

I am ready

For the offense

Never verbal am I

Physical, physical, physical.

I am psycho, I am pissed, I am thrown.

She says that she is not scared.

I will show her yet.

Have you seen the movie

'Death Becomes Her?'

Well, Death Becomes Them.

Shard in the Heart

The Battalion Fights

We had a contract.

Take your bird, I'll take my contract.

The SHOW goes on.

It goes on, it goes on, it goes on without you.

Deceit and lies.

Everybody's FOOL.

Stand ALONE.

Stand ASIDE.

The Battalion FIGHTS!

Shard in the Heart

On My Nelly

Yelling, screaming, thrashing

I hear it every day.

I don't understand it.

I hate him.

I hate all of them.

I'll never talk of him again.

The psychedelic cigarettes don't even help me.

I can't get away.

I try to make things better.

I care not.

I yell yes.

I am angry yes.

Bridge is falling.

Grass is burning.

Trees are bleeding.

I thought they were my friend.

But they are not.

Papadums are crackling.

My jacket is flaking.

I am so angry.

I might as well hear them out.

    I need a long white one.

Shard in the Heart

I won't cry, I won't yell.

Never submissive usually.

I can't concentrate.

Words will never utter.

The hate I feel.

I care for no one.

No one is on my side.

That's because I am a bitch.

And I might as well knock them out.

Plotting against me, hate trembles

In my throat,

Which is sore.

He is even counteracting an attack.

All Signs Lie

You're a Gemini, a Sagittarius, a Leo, a Scorpio,

But you're always a scorpion.

Your words sting me deep.

Slander, libel, malice- it's all the same to me.

You can't kill my spirit.

You can't kill my business.

I still rise.

I am speaking.

I am writing.

I am publishing.

I am bringing home that bling bling,

'Cause you ain't no thing, thing.

Shard in the Heart

The Trail of Abuse

Because there were records,

I had no choice but to see

the trail of abuse

he had left on

others

.

Shard in the Heart

Heartbreak

"You're leaving so soon
Never had a chance to bloom
But you were so quick
To change your tune
Don't look back
If I'm a weight around your neck
'Cos if you don't need me
I don't need you"

(Keane)

Shard in the Heart

Hidden Inside

There's a shadow in my mind.

I wish you could see this.

I could whisper into your ear

And utter my pain.

The mist surrounds me.

I withdraw

And cower on the staircase.

I want to tell you my history.

But I will only tell you

If you forgive me.

Shard in the Heart

Aaron?

After a year and a half . . .

It's all over.

It began so long ago.

He was with a boy wearing Naf Naf.

I was with my best mate,

And he with his.

It was a cool summer night,

Our meeting was fate.

We saw each other off and on,

Usually when I needed somebody,

Somebody to be my friend.

He stopped me from leaving.

I never knew much about him.

Why he was in a home?

Or why he never let me play with his bone?

Maybe he thought it was a sin?

But now he's gone.

I found out he cheated.

So, our relationships completed.

OOH what a moron!

Shard in the Heart

I'm not sad.

I only used him anyway.

I found out he was gay.

And I have someone else,

Who is just as bad.

I'll Be Your Forever Friend and

No More

With all my might

I must say . . .

Don't be daft,

Or be so gay.

For now is not the time

For us to be together.

Departure will be forth soon,

And love be lost forever,

That is if it was,

Meant to be . . .

But it is not.

A relationship

Would have to be forgot.

Don't mention a word.

Don't mention a phrase

About my decision.

Do not be sad.

Do not sorrow cos I'll be your friend,

Today and tomorrow.

Shard in the Heart

There is yet another

Issue to resolve.

Do not kiss and tell

My friend

Or you'll lose all love.

I pray to thee,

Find another

And leave me be.

There's no hope

For such as us.

I'll see you later.

Don't make a fuss.

An Aside

As tears stream down my face, I hear a whisper in my head telling me to get over it. That is simply a message in my head. The message in my heart yearns for a great relief. I know that there must be more. Each year represents one second that I spent in his company. I have a lot of crying to catch up on. I don't want the feeling to end. Does he know? Does he feel the same way I do? Will he ever? Inside sources tell me to give up. This is going to be a hard one to get over. Never in my lifetime did I think that I would experience something so unbearable. I can concentrate on nothing else until I release or express this tragedy or comedy.

Regrets?

As I sit in the cold sardine can van.

I can hear their voices laughing.

Are they laughing at me?

Who cares?

Who cares if I wasted two entire years of my life on him?

Why did I say wasted?

I learned some pretty neat stuff from that scrub.

Jealousy rages through me like a knife,

A knife stabbing my self-esteem.

Is she jealous of me?

Why are they so happy together?

I don't regret breaking it off with him.

What I regret is that I never ruined his life first.

Why am I alone?

Without a boyfriend or even a playboy?

He's not all that great, I'll grant you that.

Shard in the Heart

Why can't I just be happy for them?

They DESERVE EACHOTHER!

Does he ever think of me?

Wondering what I've been up to lately.

Wondering why I treat all guys like dirt,

Except for a select few.

Does he remember our moments?

Did he save my letters?

I hope not.

Who am I kidding? –

Surely not myself.

Shard in the Heart

Why Do I Not Feel Fulfilled?

There's something missing.

Why do I not feel fulfilled?

I should at least feel positive.

The cold opaque pit grows inside of my innermost feeling.

Did I feel happy before he came along?

Yes. No, not really . . .

I was lonely.

I wanted more than a lover.

I wanted to connect.

In the beginning, he was there for me.

We connected, really connected.

Life was perfect,

Or at least felt it.

Why do I not feel fulfilled?

Shard in the Heart

Now I feel alone again.

I have a potential boyfriend.

I have lots of money.

Been accepted to college.

Why do I not feel fulfilled?

He won't apologize.

This is my emptiness.

I strive to release my weakness.

But now everyone says- I AM FREE.

Why do I not feel fulfilled?

Maybe He's Just a Jerk

I waited so long for him to come to me.

That I couldn't believe the tree

That he kissed me under.

Nothing could be more fun.

Then in return,

We return to the ROTTEN HELL OF LIFE,

Where he pretends it never happened.

I know it did.

I know it happened because I was there,

Under the tree that he kissed me.

As the only witness,

I wait in silence,

And ponder the facts of life.

Does he like me or not?

Or are we just friends?

I guess it wasn't meant to be,

Shard in the Heart

Because the tree was fake.

It was plastic,

Just like the kisses and feelings,

From his side anyway.

♫ **Untitled** ♫

Chorus:

He doesn't know what he's doing to her

He doesn't know how she feels

He doesn't know her pain and anguish

He doesn't know X3

The pain and anguish on the moonlit night

Have broken her heart many times

It's all the same

It's broken again

He doesn't know

The cold wind blows again

Chorus

Shard in the Heart

The sadness she feels on the moonlit night

Have squeezed her heart again

The same feeling

She's been feeling again

He doesn't know

It's happened to her again

Chorus

Her best friend cares more now than ever before

She knows how she feels

She's the one who cares now

When he doesn't know again

He doesn't know

He doesn't care, it's all the same again

Chorus

How she feels . . .

Jealousy

My stomach reeling,

The anticipation feeling,

I thought he was mine,

Even though we were drunk with wine.

Just friends, it's childish.

We behaved badly,

And now, I'm a jealous bitch.

The rage, I exercise with great patience.

I want him back,

He is mine.

But he wants her,

I thought he liked me guess I was wrong.

I want to cry,

The inhale and exhale won't release my frustration.

How can they be such traitors?

I could never do that to him.

Shard in the Heart

She

She can give you pleasure.

But I can give you pleasure for eternity.

She can give you satisfaction,

But I can give you bliss.

Like two jigsaw pieces,

We fit together properly.

It makes absolute sense,

For you to choose her,

Why don't you contemplate this choice?

When I came to you,

You stole my soul.

If you aren't sure,

Give me my soul back.

Fuck her and get it over with.

I know you want me,

Shard in the Heart

Our combination is congruent.

You can make love to me,

But you can only fuck her.

So bite me!

Yearning

One sweet night in your arms,

Left me with no regrets.

Haven't met anyone like you,

You're amazing!

We parted after a long weekend,

I had hoped it would be more,

But you were just a friend.

The struggle I was almost able to bear.

And then I came back,

Once more,

Just to hold your jaw in my hands and

Kiss your gentle lips.

I tried to stop myself,

But you're irresistible.

I found myself,

Falling into your embrace once more.

Shard in the Heart

You said you have feelings for me.

You also have feelings for your dog.

What's the point in loving you,

When there's no love returned?

Inspiration

"I was made to slay them
Ten thousand hours
I'm so damn close I can taste it
On some Malcolm Gladwell
David-Bowie-meets-Kanye shit
This is dedication
A life lived for art is never a life wasted"

(Macklemore)

Shard in the Heart

Roar of a Warrior

Every little piece of that puzzle in my life

It falls together, it falls together.

Protect the cubs, protect the niblings.

The jungle is shaking out the rats in the nest.

Sitting atop the mountain of tasks,

I can see a pattern of predator on prey.

I'll send a growl, I'll send a message.

The zoo awaits the ROAR of a WARRIOR.

A glinted fang shines, glee and malice settle in

But with diamond hands they wait.

Not a moment too soon, The ROAR of a WARRIOR,

These tines of fate are too thick to change.

But they'll be fine; the cubs, the zoo, and the rest of the story too.

Shard in the Heart

Crohn's

I know I don't feel good, but just for this moment,

Let me open my eyes and sit up.

This is all I ask of me.

Just in this moment, I will take a drink of water.

Maybe I could take my pills now.

This is all I ask of me.

> Once my pills are taken the urge to empty my bladder and bowels overwhelms me. I grab my phone and stumble into the bathroom.

While I suffer, I distract myself with messages of humor and sadness.

My mind has awakened.

> Once the suffering and cleanup are complete, I realize that food would be a good idea.

> Just for this moment I will go downstairs and prepare cereal, for it is the only food that my belly does not hate.

Shard in the Heart

Please allow me to make this meal. This is all I ask for now.

Just for this moment, I'll shovel mouthfuls of food in my face. For the truth is, last night I couldn't eat dinner. I was too sick to eat.

Now that my hunger has been satisfied, I am cold. Especially in my hands and feet. The cold is pain. I am dressed warmly in pajamas and slipper socks, yet I am frigid.

Just for now, instead of crawling back into a warm bed, I will begin the process of washing my face. The standing will help my feet and hands. The warm water will help my hands. I am not promising anything.

Just for today, I am only washing my face.

Learner

I love how being a learner takes you to places you never thought you could go.

How hope can guide you to places where synchronicity lies.

How just being in the presence of greatness inspires you to want more.

How it inspires you to do more.

Show others what you have learned.

Shard in the Heart

Every Lady

Every lady is a princess,

Though she doesn't feel that way.

Every day is stressful,

She must try to stay and play.

I feel I could fly if I wanted.

I think I even have.

But if I let life bog me down,

I can't see the beauty portrayed.

The dew in the grass is relaxing.

The coffee is very hot.

When I close my eyes tightly,

I can see the little sparkles.

A suit is not a gown.

And a gown is just for fun.

It feels more free than butterflies,

And I feel free in every one.

A lady is a princess,

Whether or not she knows.

The love she feels for nature,

Shows so much she glows.

Shard in the Heart

Who Are Our Parents?

They are not always biological,

But they love us just the same.

They are honored and obeyed.

We don't always do as they say.

They are our best teachers,

Because they are patient yet firm.

They show us how we can make our life easier.

But the problem is getting us to listen.

Their wisdom guides us daily.

As their lessons echo in our minds.

They take care of us when we need them most.

Whether we be ill or distraught or misguided.

They surprise us and encourage us,

With tales of experience and faith.

Most of all, they honor us by being the best gift gods could ever give.

We are grateful to have you as parents.

Shard in the Heart

Light the Way

Take a deep breath, choose your words.

Take a deep breath, you don't gotta rush this.

Take a deep breath, take deep breath, take a deep breath.

Learn about the life that you wanna lead.

Surrounded by the people who love you.

Surrounded by those who have fought to light the way.

You don't gotta suffer by your lonesome.

Cause when you really need it.

Take a deep breath, take a deep breath, take a deep breath…

And then, you, you and the people who love you.

Will help you light a new path into the life that you've always wanted to lead.

Just take a deep breath, a deep breath…. And you and the people who looooove you….. Will take a deep breath, take a deep breath, deep breath.

Shard in the Heart

Ode to Diana

Hate is useless.

Walk the battlefield.

How can you sit back and do nothing?

Be a hero for someone you don't know.

Do your part to make the change.

Do you see the truth?

Fight for what matters ~*

Food, shelter, clothing, freedom, and safety.

Could you give up your one true love to save the world?

Maybe people aren't always good.

Maybe bad people are bad because they are treated badly.

The only way to save the world is with love.

The only way to save the world is with courage.

The courage to be Diana Prince . . .

Shard in the Heart

Love

"I wrote the song two hours before we met
I didn't know your name or what you looked like yet
Oh, I could have stayed at home and gone to bed
I could have gone to see a film instead
You might have changed your mind and seen your friends
Life could have been very different but then
Something changed"

(Pulp)

Shard in the Heart

Truth

Am I really beautiful?

Does my hair shine in the sun?

Do my eyes twinkle like stars?

Or are you just having your fun?

Shard in the Heart

Untitled

To the only one I ever loved,

Please bear a moment with me.

While I write this short quatrain

And tell my love for thee.

Shard in the Heart

It Happened Only Yesterday

Having only met you

It feels so strange to say.

Feeling like I've known you

Every night and every day.

I wish each day would last forever

So we could hold each other.

Night and day, "forever" you say

And never have to stray.

Your thoughts are in my mind.

Your mind is in my head.

I fear it's clear to say

I want you in my bed.

Later is not forever my dear,

Cause forever never ends.

So rush to me with caring arms

And stop us from dead ends.

Shard in the Heart

Give Me a Reason

What did I do to deserve your love?

You fill me with happiness.

And fill my heart with love.

Is it a gift from up above?

Your sweet embrace,

The smile on your face,

Are all gifts for me,

And they take me to another place.

How can I justify your tender caress?

Or the giggle you make when I wear a dress?

Your smooth hand on my soft cheek,

Without you, life is bleak.

Did I run away to be with you?

Or am I still me?

Should I jump up and down for joy?

Or would you call me insane?

Shard in the Heart

How do I say, "I love you?"

Without spoiling those three words.

Please tell me what I did to thee,

To deserve a love so free.

Shall I see you today?

Will you touch me so lovingly?

With passion in an embrace?

Or just smile softly as you look upon my face.

Tell me now . . .

What did I do to deserve your love?

If I Gave You a Piece of Paper,

Would You Scribble or Draw?

Expressing these words on the sheet of a page,

Is painful only because I care for you so much.

With a tremendous sigh, I release the pain, the anxiety

I was misguided to think I meant anything to you.

It was only a fling.

With much more hunger than I have ever felt.

I saw the page turn over,

Onto your lap.

Write to me.

Release your confusion.

I will feel each depression in each pore.

I am the paper.

You are the pen.

Shard in the Heart

Is there any hope?

Do you care?

How do you feel?

Write on me.

Prom Date

I'm sitting here, thinking of you.

All alone and cold

I want you by my side through new & old

I asked that special question, just an hour ago.

My feelings are down upon the floor and below.

Your sun-kissed blonde hair,

Your soft cherry lips,

The muscles in your back

To match your slim tan hips.

Please say yes, or I'll be a mess.

I've got the dress, now don't be a pest.

Tell me now what I need to know.

My California king needs a California queen,

A date for the prom.

Shard in the Heart

Untitled

Sometimes at night you wake me up just to cuddle.
You put your toe beans in my palm and press gently
like we are holding hands. The vibration of your
purring calms my heart. My peanut butter cat, Carter
Bear.

Shard in the Heart

Lust

"I bet you want the goodies.
Bet you thought about it.
Got you all hot and bothered.
Maybe cause I talk about it.
Looking for the goodies
Keep on lookin' cause they stay in the jar"

(Ciara)

Shard in the Heart

Naughty Name Poem

Easy

Lips

Leaning

Every

Naughty

Existence

In

Corners

Kinky

Holding

Only

Lips

Tightly

Shard in the Heart

Animal Desire

We're both so different,

And yet, I feel,

A love so strong,

Burning in my chest.

It's like an animal,

Uncaged only when you're around.

When I feel down,

I feel your presence.

Yet I argue.

And I'll argue till

My dying day.

That's just the way I am.

Some things you say,

Hurt deep inside,

And I want to run away,

Though I still want to be with you.

Shard in the Heart

Don't let me stray.

Please make me stay,

And all your wishes,

Will be fulfilled with my desires.

Dirty Wife

The dirty wife is not one to be reckoned with.

She is not one who can become clean with oils, soaps, and fragrances.

She will not allow her calloused exterior to be scrubbed away.

The dirty wife keeps it all to herself.

She does not let her neighbors know about her filth.

She keeps it hidden in a drawer with silken cloths.

The dirty wife only knows one companion.

She lets her true self be known only to the one she trusts the most.

In a place where she is free to be the Goddess that she is.

The dirty wife knows that her secret is safe between 400 count pieces.

She knows that what is dirty cannot be thrown in the hamper.

It can only be harvested, nurtured, and expressed behind her locked doors.

Shard in the Heart

Untitled

As you devour my body

There is an electric shock

That passes from my neck to my clit

Finding a void for my well being

Shard in the Heart

Ode to a Confidant

The soft anticipation of his smile

Made me want to kiss him with the passion I have never felt.

After waiting a while

I discovered that romance would make our friendship melt.

It's not easy to restrain myself around his enthusiastic being.

I thought that maybe I should go for the chance

And hope that he was feeling what I was feeling

And go for a peck on the cheek at the high school dance.

The fun at the park.

The fun at the rope.

The fun of the dark.

Help, I need to restrain!

Call the pope.

I didn't want to ruin our friendship

And take the chance of losing our great trust.

Without his friendship I would flip.

Please help me restrain – **I must.**

Shard in the Heart

I Could Do That Too

She breathes deeply.

I could breathe deeply for you too.

With the caress of a hand,

I could breathe deeply for you.

The nerve of her breast entrances.

I could heave entrancingly for you too.

With the brush of a hand,

I could heave entrancingly for you.

She moans like a wild beast.

I could moan beastly for you, too.

With the thrust of your tongue,

I could moan beastly for you.

She whispers passionate sighs.

I could whisper passionately for you too.

With the nibble of my nipple,

I could whisper passionately for you.

If only you let me . . .

Shard in the Heart

Pandemic

"Oh, people like us
We gotta stick together
Keep your head up
Nothing lasts forever
Here's to the damned, to the lost and forgotten
It's hard to get high when you're living on the bottom

Oh-woah, oh-woah
We are all misfits living in a world on fire"

(Bomer)

Shard in the Heart

A Breath for India

All along the oxygen train

They beg concentrators,

They fight for the right to live.

The government played with their lives.

A political dance spouting economic prosperity.

A festival of belief spouting protection by their gods.

All borders are manmade.

How many will be saved?

With the arrival of the oxygen train.

How many broken hearts are left to burn?

Did you lose your whole family or just your daughter?

All along the oxygen train.

The train was late.

2 crore, 2 million, 2 many zeros.

The planes coming in want to be heroes.

Shard in the Heart

The cheat codes were on

But time ran out

All along the oxygen train.

What I Would Give

My first kiss - the boy who played Care Bears and My Little Pony with me.

Knowing how it feels to float - the gentle kisses of water lap upon my back.

Blue cheese in all forms - making iceberg lettuce into a gourmet delight.

All of Prince's music - every song he has written and every song he will write in the afterlife.

Fresh peaches – a smell and taste so unique that the olfactory confuses it with sensuality.

All movies by John Hughes - we don't deserve them if we can't put humanity first.

I would give all of this and much more to end the pandemic.

What would you give?

Shard in the Heart

Summer 2021

Have your fun now while you may,
The delta variants on its way.
A summer cough and cold,
Only the vaccinated grow old.

Travel now or travel never,
Stay apart or stay together.
Your bubble get bigger,
Your bubble fades away.

It's too late, crying from bed,
You see the reaper with dread.
Was it all in your head?
Facebook was all you read.

Soon you'll be dead,
Misinformation you spread.
Should I give a damn about you?
You started an insurrection coup.

NO - FUCK THAT!

Shard in the Heart

Politics

"All you people up there in City Hall,
You're fuckin' it up for the people that's in the streets.
This is a song for the people in the streets,
Not the people City Hall.
All you motherfuckers in the streets it's time to rise up,
Come along children and fuckin' rise!"

(TenaciousD)

Shard in the Heart

Officer Fanone

We got a 10-33.
What's that to me?
They're fighting for democracy.
MAGA hats don't know the gravity.

Kill him with his own gun, SURGE!
No humanity, unconscious, SCOURGE!
Up shit's creek without protection.
I have kids! Only a deflection.

They say they back the blue,
But they started this coup.
A skull crusher INSURRECTION.
Nightmares haunt daily introspection.

Shard in the Heart

Love Letter from a MAGANAZI

I'm a sadist.
I keep dreaming about these people.
Why couldn't they stay longer?
God damn.
What they all meant to us,
They're unrecognizable now.
I miss how I felt when I was around them.
I wish there was a way they could accept us,
the way we are now but
there's no way they could do that.
It's really hard
when you lose someone you've known
for so long.
I'm sorry
WE
have to go through this
over and over again.
It's worse than if someone just died.
A person,
An energy,
A trust,
It just goes away.
Does the friendship grow
or does it wither and die?[iii]

Shard in the Heart

Consequences

August seventeenth

Mark's the day.

Where no plans were made.

Guy asks girl.

She agrees.

Awareness is not upon them.

AIDS and pregnancy are the fear

Of the young and smart.

No one thinks of the bad

When they have "it" on the brain.

School intrigues both.

Neither carry jobs.

Curiosity overcomes them.

Later . . .

They have gone too far.

Fears surround us.

Shard in the Heart

Ones they should know.

Ones they should care about

But . . .

Hormones rule their bodies.

All fears are black.

But an unborn child with AIDS

Is one to mourn for.

But no one cares.

People say it happens every day.

I know.

Crying cannot change the past.

So next time think of the future.

Egg Yolk

Bust it, bust it

It's all yellow & yucky.

Bust it, bust it

It's all funky & mellow.

Bust it, bust it

It's different from the white.

Bust it, bust it

Mix it in with the white, white toast.

Bust it, bust it

It's different from the white.

Bust it, bust it

Repeat all x 2

Shard in the Heart

We Almost Lost

And the whole world watched.

And they called for takeout.

And they sent a meme.

And they cried a little.

And their niece became their nephew.

And their nephew became their niece.

And so, Auntie and Uncle put a rainbow in the yard.

And someone with a pickup moved in.

And he put up his Trump sign from 2016.

And the man with diabetes put out his Biden sign.

And some held up signs for a haircut.

And some held up signs to remind us that they are not 3/5ths of a person.

And some fought to keep parents and kids together in cages.

And Democracy faded away,

With each executive order,

Shard in the Heart

With each vote in the dark,

With each stolen vote.

And I tried to stay awake.

And it was like a miracle.

And the red states turned into blue.

And I felt hope again.

And we cried together.

And we danced in the streets.

And as the COVID cases grew,

And the president-elect took stage,

We knew the dark winter was coming.

And we'd prepared for it.

But it was no longer the darkest timeline.

And we knew it wasn't the end of our story.

Sisterhood YOU

Wearing pants now because of you.

Fought for me cause it's through.

Cut my hair now because of you,

Wear long or cut it crew.

Work at home now because of you,

Independent as fuck it's true.

Rallies and emails fill their cue,

Won't let up now 'cause of you.

Don't go to bed hungry because of you,

Havin' food stamps 'n disability too.

Got an education because of you,

Gonna use it and get my due.

Shard in the Heart

It ain't over 'cause of you.

Gonna keep fighting you know it's true.

Fought so hard our power grew.

I'm alive because of you.

Suffragette you know it's true.

AOC knows what to do.

Stay woke daily cause of you.

It's my body, I won't be moved.

This sisterhood ain't afraid bugaboo.

We be fightin' your January 6th coup.

Less Racist Now

Was it OK when he was afraid because he saw more people of color?

Was it OK when he told a joke about an apple tree in all white company?

Was it OK when he repeated the scenes of violence for his sick pleasure?

Was it OK when he was expressing his first amendment right?

No - but I knew it was wrong when she said, "That day really changed him, he met people of all colors and now he's less racist."

Shard in the Heart

Scotland

"Memories will never last my life's fading, trying to remember the rhymes and notes, to a song that I never wrote about, lump swelling in my throat, realise I'm going to be looking back at those days laughing when we never were afraid."

(BabyYaga)

Shard in the Heart

The Change in Cider

In a vision

Of near unconsciousness

I raise my hand

High above many others.

Like a cold glass of cider

I am to be drunken slowly

But with much eagerness

To be appreciated.

All perception is disrupted

In a place where people are more free.

I am like that glass of cider

In a bar full of many people.

I can make people shine.

I can make people whine.

I just make them free

To do as they wish.

No restrictions.

Shard in the Heart

Remembering

The pumping beat running through my soul,

Takes me back to Flicks^{iv}

The place is so lovely,

And so free.

A small wrapper or a

Song heard on the radio

Takes me back to the place I miss.

Why can't I go there?

Every ounce of my body

Wants to return to the homeland

Not where I was born

But to the place where I belong.

I must return someday

To release these energies

A small vacation or maybe a lifetime.

I must go to Scotland soon.

Shard in the Heart

Ode to ASA

The mental hospital that sits on a hill,

The old Edzell bus driver, his name was Bill.

The school where you can be who you are

And where you have to be a senior to drive a car.

Where the computer lab is full at lunchtime,

And where skipping school's the biggest crime.

Where 11,000 pounds pays for nothing,

And where education finally means something.

With ice cream duets in the hall,

And Bon Accords the only mall.

We're a class unique yet wise,

The principal's a dimple - surprise, surprise!

Shard in the Heart

Ode to Sanity

I searched the hills of Scottish heather

I found you not.

I walked the concrete steps of life

To try to encounter a passion like yours.

You were right in front of me,

I saw you not.

Your pacifying blue eyes,

Your smooth crimson lips,

Your long mane,

All entranced me into your seduction.

And I gave you body-wrenching passion,

Where I found home.

And now the clock is broken.

No longer can I feel your rough hands on my silky breasts.

The passion of our profiles was divine.

It's not over yet.

You will yearn for my emptiness once more.

Shard in the Heart

Foreign Country

Part I

The cool breeze has a warmth.

As I furrow my brow

I need to escape.

I feel conspiracy at my workplace.

The loneliness is found.

As I feel lost and discriminated,

The inevitable is coming,

As I give forth to my sentence.

Only the breeze is my comfort.

I wallow in my pity.

Never mind that I bust my butt

To prove my capabilities.

The only triumph that is left

Is to remain dignified

Throughout my pain.

Shard in the Heart

Part II

Head filled with clouds, in the clouds

Never bothered

Am I without a song

To sing as I cry

And think of nothing

So lovely as this emptiness

Shard in the Heart

Part III

The endless chatter

Of formidable destinies

Of friends and foes

Is it stopping me?

Is it holding me down?

Is it something I want?

An excuse to remain the same

An only friend found through

A lovers' relationship

Wanting to savor a friendship

I chose to be gossiped about

And live inside the endless chatter

Shard in the Heart

No Chlorine

A seventeen-year-old girl and an eighteen-year-old
Playing in the pool of nature.
The girls felt refreshed
As they sat in the cool embrace of the Edzell River.

As they talked things came into focus.
It wasn't just boring teenage stuff either.
They connected.
No one know about them.

Drenching journey
with seaweed

The bitter water made them realize
That life is more than a swim.
More than a swim in a bleach

Infested pool.

Life is about friendship,

Love and understanding.

It was a bonding that the two
Would never forget.

Each memory held in their hearts
Like a locket of stone.

Shard in the Heart

Old Bread & Angry Bees

Leaving is like a piece of old bread.

Although your life is stale and moldy

It is comfortable.

That's why the bacteria moves in.

You don't want to scrape the bacteria off.

And you don't want to throw the bread away,

It would be a waste of bread.

Leaving is like an angry bee.

A bee is happy until you control it.

A bee is happy to pollinate the flowers.

A bee is angry until you annoy it.

Then it's an angry bee.

One that complains and stings anything in its sight.

An angry bee can cause a lot of pain.

Leaving is changing and adapting.

It's the evolution of all living things.

We are all afraid of leaving

Because it involves changing.

Shard in the Heart

You can show your feelings like a piece of old bread or like an angry bee

But we will still have to leave.

Me

"Never was a cornflake girl

Thought it was a good solution

Hanging with the raisin girls

She's gone to the other side

Giving us the yo heave ho

Things are getting kind of gross

And I go at sleepy time"

(Amos)

Shard in the Heart

7 of Cups

Unanswered aspirations,
Attentive admiration,
Aberrant oddments,
Irregular anomalies,
Atrocity antics,
Guile artifice,
Drink me.

Shard in the Heart

Dancing

Rhythm   Trembling

Inexhaustible   Shaking

Energy   Sweat

Speed   Pressure

Pumping   Moaning

Insanity   Chills

Pleasure
Comfort

Frustration
Fulfilled

Anxiety
Relaxation

Shard in the Heart

Untitled

Exhaustion fazes my eyes

A blink once or twice

To keep me awake

I shouldn't sit in this

Comfortable seat and

Drift away to a show

Where I, only know my dreams

Shard in the Heart

Shard in the Heart

¿Cuantas Horas Pará Mi?

Hay diez y seis horas

Bueno, yo digo

¿Dónde está la letra?

¿Dónde qué?

La letra

(Estoy bien my friend)

La letra para adiós, amigos

Yo tengo lo

Dame lo

Aquí dice no hay un cuerpo

Es bueno

No hay insectos en el mundo

Yo muerto

Al fin.

Shard in the Heart

The End

It's the end
So completed, so complete
The last conspires
I'm not a liar
I'm only coming round the bend
So, it's only the end for me

They all have to suffer
I reach for the pill
They all have to suffer
As I run down the hill
So completed, so complete

Al fin, Al fin, the end, al fin.
¿Cómo estás?
Estoy bien mi amiga
Porque es el fin
Porque es el fin

I reach for the pill
To find the hill
The end, my friend
Al fin

La salsa dice, "Hola amiga, hola."
"I yo dice, "Al fin, al fin, estoy al fin."

I reach for the pill, to find the hill
The end, my friend, Al fin.

Shard in the Heart

Miscellaneous

Shard in the Heart

Life is not an untimed test.

- Gandalf Clarke

***

What kind of ear medicine does a Ferengi use?

Oo-moxacilin

Shard in the Heart

Him: How's that fibro flare?

Me: How's that attention deficit disorder?

Him: I'm on speed; you're on slow.

Acknowledgments

I would like to thank my writing team at Battalion-13 Entertainment Inc. for pushing me outside my comfort zone. Dawnsk, my mini me, for reading my mind; and bringing order to chaos. Rob for helping me delve deeper into subject matter. Gandalf for being my sounding board and my sanity; without his love, the *Shard in My Heart* would never have healed.

Shard in the Heart

About the Author

Ellen Clarke lives in Frederick, Maryland near the Catoctin Mountains with her husband Gandalf and her three tortoiseshell cats. She enjoys bicycling along the C & O Canal forged by her great grandfather, Jorge. Ellen is a writer of fiction and recipes; she is an actor for Battalion-13 Entertainment where she and her friends produce a full-cast audio sci-fi horror story podcast. She also narrates audiobooks and discusses Crohn's, magic, leadership, and action figures as a YouTube Vlogger. Please visit the company's website at:

www.battlion13hq.com

Shard in the Heart

Bibliography

Amos, Tori. *YouTube*. Vers. Official US Version. 10 January 2014.
Uproxx Indie Mixtape. Video. 4 August 2021.
<https://www.youtube.com/watch?v=w_HA5Czhtx4>.

Atwood, Margaret.
*https://en.wikipedia.org/wiki/Power_Politics_(poetry_colle
ction)*. 7 July 2020. Wikipedia. 30 July 2021.

BabyYaga. *YouTube*. Vers. Official. 19 December 2019. Video. 4
August 2021.
<https://www.youtube.com/watch?v=AgQLe-Ig_64>.

Battalion-13. *Battalion-13: The Podcast*. 21 May 2018. Podcast.
29 July 2021. <www.battalion13hq.com>.

Bomer, Matt. Ed. The Watcher. Vers. Scene. n.d. Video. 4 August
2021.
<https://www.youtube.com/watch?v=1vojrVQeOYI>.

Ciara. n.d. Video. 4 August 2021.
<https://www.youtube.com/watch?v=WCMQlcRi34Y>.

Eickholt, Ellen S. "Reaction to Rejection." Sullivan, C. *Into the
Unknown*. Ownings Mills: National Library of Poetry,
1996. Book, Poem.

Keane. *Keane*. 11 June 2020. Video. 30 7 2021.
<https://www.youtube.com/watch?v=c2uUT2bzp7Q>.

Macklemore, Ryan Lewis. *Macklemore*. 4 January 2013. Video. 4
January 2013. <
https://www.youtube.com/watch?v=lxZPNXRT2fQ>.

Masson, James. *Evening Telegraph*. n.d. Article. 4 August 2021.
<https://www.eveningtelegraph.co.uk/2014/06/04/back-to-
the-80s-how-flicks-nightclub-in-brechin-h>.

MCR, My Chemical Romance. Vers. Official . n.d. YouTube
    Video:. 30 July 2021.
    <https://www.youtube.com/watch?v=RRKJiM9Njr8>.

Morrisette, Alanis. *Alanis, Morrisette.* 7 November 2014. Video.
    30 July 2021.
    <https://www.youtube.com/watch?v=kiiYS2vLD5Y>.

Pulp. 23 September 2018. Video. 30 July 2021. <
    https://www.youtube.com/watch?v=zxm_3J3r5rM>.

TenaciousD. n.d. Borogroove. . Video. 4 August 2021.
    <https://www.youtube.com/watch?v=Co2Zt615P5M>.

Various. *Wikipedia.* 30 April 2021. Wiki. 30 July 2021.
    <https://en.wikipedia.org/wiki/Laotong>.

—. *Wikipedia.* 8 July 2021. Wiki. 4 August 2021.

End Notes

---

[i] The most commonly accepted meaning is that a "hollaback girl" responds positively to the "catcalls" or hollers of men, but it might mean to Stefani that she would rather take the initiative and "step it up"…" (Various, Hollaback_Girl.)

[ii] This poem won several awards. – (Eickholt)

[iii] Written by both Gandalf Clarke and Ellen Clarke

[iv] Flicks was a nightclub in Brechin, Scotland. (Masson)

Made in the USA
Coppell, TX
30 September 2021